CAKE POPS

HELEN ATTRIDGE AND ABBY FOY

PHOTOGRAPHS BY LIS PARSONS

spruce

An Hachette UK Company
www.hachette.co.uk

First published in Great Britain in 2012 by Spruce
a division of Octopus Publishing Group Ltd
Endeavour House, 189 Shaftesbury Avenue, London, WC2H 8JY
www.octopusbooks.co.uk
www.octopusbooksusa.com

Copyright © Octopus Publishing Group Ltd 2012

Distributed in the USA by Hachette Book Group USA
237 Park Avenue, New York, NY 10017, USA

Distributed in Canada by Canadian Manda Group
165 Dufferin Street, Toronto, Ontario, Canada, M6K 3H6

All rights reserved. No part of this work may be reproduced or utilized
in any form or by any means, electronic or mechanical, including
photocopying, recording, or by any information storage and retrieval
system, without the prior written permission of the publisher.

Helen Attridge and Abby Foy assert the moral right to be identified
as the authors of this work

ISBN 978-1-84601-402-4

Printed and bound in China

10 9 8 7 6 5 4 3 2 1

CONSULTANT PUBLISHER Sarah Ford
SENIOR EDITOR Leanne Bryan
COPY-EDITOR Nicole Foster
DESIGN MANAGER Eoghan O'Brien
DESIGNER Clare Barber
PHOTOGRAPHER Lis Parsons
PRODUCTION MANAGER Katherine Hockley
PRODUCTION CONTROLLER Sarah Kramer

CONTENTS

4   Introduction
5   Making cake pops

CLASSIC POPS

8   Simple chocolate pops
10   Simple pretty pops
12   Chocolate cake pops
14   Chocolate-dipped strawberry pops
16   Spring flower pops
18   Summer dress pops

CELEBRATION POPS

20   Bright balloon pops
22   Party hat pops
24   Tea set pops
26   Cocktail pops
28   Cowgirl hat pops
30   Mr. & Mrs. Pops
32   Wedding cake pops
34   Baby carriage pops

FESTIVE POPS

36   Valentine's champagne bottle pops
38   Sparkly Valentine's heart pops
40   Chocolate Easter Egg pops
42   Sparkly pumpkin pops
44   Bat pops
46   Stocking pops
48   Christmas cracker pops

ANIMAL POPS

50   Teddy bear pops
52   Penguin pops
54   Duck family pops
56   Whale pops
58   Parrot pops
60   Piggy pops
62   Caterpillar pops

64   Conversions / Glossary /
Source List / Acknowledgments

INTRODUCTION

When Helen's sister-in-law Veronica moved from the United States to the UK and asked where she could buy some "popcakes," we had no idea what she meant. However, after researching American Web sites online, we fell in love with them.

We have always worked in catering and love to be creative, and almost immediately we started experimenting with different flavors and designs. We had so much fun, and the response to our first creations was so overwhelming, that we decided to open Popcake Kitchen.

This book includes cake pops that involve a range of decorating skills, and while we hope to encourage everyone to try the "advanced" level pop designs, we get just as much pleasure from producing the "simple" examples.

The only thing we enjoy more than baking (and eating!) our pops is seeing other people's reactions when they discover the unique treats we have made for them. We're sure that after trying our pops for yourself, you too will enjoy treating your family and friends for years to come … HAPPY POPPING!

MAKING CAKE POPS

The great thing about cake pops is that the baked cake doesn't need to look perfect! Our recipe will deliver cake pops with very little effort and can be adapted to create several yummy flavors.

BASIC VANILLA CAKE POP RECIPE

This recipe makes slightly more cake pops than in our design guides so you will have a few to experiment with—or make extra, because they won't last long!

PREPARE AHEAD Preheat the oven to 350°F (180°C). Line an 8-inch (20-cm) baking pan with wax paper.

TO MAKE THE CAKE Place the butter and sugar in a food processor and mix on a medium speed until white and fluffy. Add the vanilla extract and mix in.

Add half the beaten eggs and flour to the mixture and combine well. Repeat with the remaining eggs and flour.

Pour the batter into the prepared pan and bake for approximately 30–35 minutes. To see if your cake is cooked, insert a fork into the center—it should come out clean.

Cool the cake on a cooling rack.

TO MAKE THE FROSTING Beat together the butter, sugar, and vanilla extract in a mixing bowl until thoroughly mixed.

FLAVOR VARIATIONS

RICH CHOCOLATE Replace ¼ cup (25 g) flour with ¼ cup (25 g) unsweetened cocoa powder. For the frosting, add 1 teaspoon unsweetened cocoa powder to the mixture, or for extra chocolate flavor add melted chocolate to taste.

ZINGY LEMON Add the juice and zest of one lemon to the butter and sugar mixture and stir. For the frosting, add the juice of half a lemon to the mixture.

FOR THE CAKE

Makes approximately 25 golf-ball-size cake pops

1¾ sticks (200 g) unsalted butter, softened

1 cup (200 g) superfine sugar

1 teaspoon vanilla extract

3 eggs, lightly beaten

Scant 2 cups (250 g) self-rising flour, sifted

FOR THE FROSTING

1 stick (125 g) unsalted butter, softened

1¾ cups (200 g) confectioners' sugar

1 teaspoon vanilla extract

MAKING THE CAKE BALLS

Break or slice the cooled cake into manageable pieces. Crumble the pieces by hand or, for a finer result, use the grater attachment in a food processor.

Using your hands, mix the frosting into the cake crumbs. Add a tablespoon at a time—you may not need it all. Too much frosting will make the pops too wet to stay on the sticks when being dipped. The mixture is ready once it holds together when rolled in your hands.

Divide the mixture and roll into balls about the size of golf balls (weighing about 1-oz/25-g), or form into the required shape for your pop design.

Once shaped, put the cake balls on a plate and cover. Place in the refrigerator for at least an hour until the mixture is firm. They can be kept, covered, in the refrigerator for up to 2 days.

YOU WILL NEED

1 bag of candy melts
Spoon, Microwavable bowl
Vegetable oil
20 cake balls
20 lollipop sticks
Toothpick

DIPPING THE CAKE POPS

Once the cake balls are firm to the touch they are ready to dip.

Empty the candy melts into a microwavable bowl and heat on medium for about 2 minutes. Stir at 20-second intervals to make sure the candy melts evenly and doesn't burn.

Stir a little vegetable oil, a tablespoon at a time, into the melted candy. This will help thin the candy and achieve a silky, workable texture. The finished candy should run off a spoon.

Remove the cake balls from the refrigerator. Dip ½ inch (1 cm) of a lollipop stick into the melt and insert into the center of a ball, going about halfway through. Be careful not to push too hard, but make sure it is in far enough to secure the ball. Let set upright (a block of Styrofoam is handy here!).

When set, dip the cake pop into the melted candy making sure it is completely covered.

Gently tap the stick on the side of the bowl to remove any excess candy. Flip the pop and tap the other side to gain a smooth, even coating. Use the pointed end of a toothpick to burst any bubbles that may appear in the candy melt when tapping.

Let dry upright. Once dipped, the cake pops will keep for 3–4 days in a cool, dry place.

DECORATING THE CAKE POPS

Now it's time to get creative! You can add all kinds of edible decorations to your pops to create simple yet effective designs. Some of our more complicated pops require a little more work but produce stunning results. Here are a few basic techniques:

- Add sprinkles while the candy melt is still wet. Take a pinch of your chosen decoration between thumb and fingers and gently sprinkle over the cake pop.

- Add edible decorations once the cake pop is dry by dabbing melted candy with a toothpick onto the surface and attaching your chosen decoration.

- Cut decorations from rolled fondant, which is very easy to work with. When rolling, lightly dust a smooth work surface with flour or cornstarch to stop it from sticking.

- Add elegant touches with piped candy. Fill a plastic pastry bag with melted candy, twist the end, and snip a small hole at the bottom. Gently squeeze the bag to release a steady stream of candy.

SHAPING CAKE POPS

Make your cake pops into weird and wonderful shapes using some of the following techniques:

- Roll the cake ball against the work surface to create a sausage shape—a great base for many pop designs.

- Angle your hands while rolling to make an egg shape.

- Push the cake ball against the work surface to produce flat edges.

SIMPLE CHOCOLATE POPS

These simple yet delicious cake pops will allow for you to learn the basic popping techniques and use readily available ingredients.

YOU WILL NEED

20 cake balls, see pages 5–6
20 lollipop sticks
Styrofoam block
Bowl
Spoon
Toothpick

DECORATION

1 bag of light cocoa candy melts
Small chocolate-coated crispy balls
   or white chocolate stars

DIFFICULTY RATING

PREPARE AHEAD Chill the cake balls in the refrigerator for 1 hour.

TO MAKE THE CAKE POPS Melt the candy melts (see page 6), dip a stick into the melted candy, and push into a cake ball. Repeat with all the sticks and cake balls. Let set. Dip each cake pop into the melted candy and tap off the excess.

TO DECORATE Sprinkle the chocolate balls, if using, over the cake pop to cover before the candy melt sets.

If you are adding the stars, let the coated cake pop dry, then dab melted candy onto the cake pop with a toothpick and attach the stars.

TIP

Sprinkle the chocolate balls over a bowl to catch the excess. You can then continue to sprinkle these over the cake pops with a spoon.

SIMPLE PRETTY POPS

These simple, pretty cake pops provide another way to learn the basic popping techniques using cake-decorating ingredients.

YOU WILL NEED

20 cake balls, see pages 5–6
20 lollipop sticks
Styrofoam block
Bowl
Spoon
Toothpick

DECORATION

1 bag of white candy melts
Tiny flower or butterfly sprinkles
  or royal icing flowers

DIFFICULTY RATING

PREPARE AHEAD Chill the cake balls in the refrigerator for 1 hour.

TO MAKE THE CAKE POPS Melt the candy melts (see page 6), dip a stick into the melted candy, and push into a cake ball. Repeat with all the sticks and cake balls. Let set. Dip each cake pop into the melted candy and tap off the excess.

TO DECORATE Gently sprinkle the tiny flower sprinkles, if using, over the top of the cake pop before the candy melt sets.

If you are adding butterfly sprinkles or royal icing flowers, dab melted candy onto the dried cake pop using a toothpick and attach your chosen decoration.

TIP

Sprinkle the decorations over a bowl to catch the excess. You can then continue to sprinkle these over the cake pops with a spoon.

CHOCOLATE CAKE POPS

These taste as good as they look, especially when made with rich chocolate cake and frosting.

20 cake balls, see pages 5–6
20 lollipop sticks
Styrofoam block
Plastic rolling pin
Knife
Plastic pastry bag
Toothpick

DECORATION

1 bag of light cocoa candy melts
9 oz (250 g) pale pink rolled
    fondant
Cornstarch
¼ bag of white candy melts
Bright pink royal icing flowers

DIFFICULTY RATING

PREPARE AHEAD Form the cake balls into cake slices: push each ball into a triangle shape, using your work surface or the side of a knife to achieve straight edges. Chill in the refrigerator for 1 hour.

TO MAKE THE CAKE POPS Melt the light cocoa candy melts (see page 6), dip a stick into the melted candy, and push into the top of a cake triangle. Repeat with all the sticks and cake triangles. Let set. Dip each cake pop into the melted candy and tap off the excess. Let the slices dry upside down in a Styrofoam block.

TO DECORATE Roll out the pink fondant to approximately ⅛ inch (2.5 mm) thick on a surface dusted with cornstarch. Place a dry cake pop onto the fondant and carefully cut around the pointed end using a knife. Roll the pop onto its outer end and cut around this, too—you will be left with a shape that resembles a rocket. Push a hole through the triangle part of the fondant (be careful to get this in the right place so that the fondant fits perfectly onto the cake pop). Slide the fondant shape down the stick of your pop and secure in place with melted candy applied with a toothpick. "Frost" all the cake pops in the same way.

Melt the white candy melts (see page 6) and use to fill the pastry bag. Twist the top and snip off a small opening at the bottom. Pipe around the center of each slice of cake using a tight zigzag motion to create the effect of cake filling.

TO FINISH Dab melted candy onto the top of the cake using a toothpick and attach a pink royal icing flower.

TIP
—

When tapping off the excess candy melt, let dribble from the pointed end of the pop to create a smooth finish on each side.

CHOCOLATE-DIPPED STRAWBERRY POPS

Yes that's a cake pop you're looking at, not a real strawberry!

YOU WILL NEED

20 cake balls, see pages 5–6
20 lollipop sticks
Toothpick
Styrofoam block
Plastic rolling pin
1-inch (2.5-cm) round
   cookie cutter
Knife
Wax paper

DECORATION

1 bag of red candy melts
3½ oz (100 g) green rolled fondant
Cornstarch
½ bag of light cocoa candy melts

DIFFICULTY RATING

PREPARE AHEAD Make the cake balls into strawberry shapes by angling your hands when rolling and slightly flattening the tops. Chill in the refrigerator for 1 hour.

TO MAKE THE CAKE POPS Melt the red candy melts (see page 6), dip a stick into the melted candy, and push into the top of a strawberry shape. Repeat with all the sticks and cake shapes. Let set. Dip each cake pop into the melted candy and tap off the excess. Working quickly, dab the wet candy with a toothpick in a random pattern to create the texture of a strawberry. Let the cake pops dry in a Styrofoam block.

To create the green stalk, roll out the fondant on a surface dusted with cornstarch to approximately ¹⁄₁₆ inch (1.2 mm) thick. Cut out 20 circles, using a 1-inch (2.5-cm) cutter, and make a hole in the middle of each with a lollipop stick. Use a knife to make the jagged starlike shape by working out from the center of the circle, leaving ½ inch (1 cm) around the hole. Dab melted candy onto the top of a strawberry using a toothpick, slide a stalk shape down the stick, and attach. Attach each stalk to a strawberry in the same way.

TO FINISH Melt the candy melts and dip in each strawberry halfway. Tap off a little excess and hold at an angle on the wax paper. Hold steady until set.

TIP
—

Lean the sticks of the chocolate-dipped strawberries against an object to make sure they all set at the same angle.

SPRING FLOWER POPS

A spring flower pop bouquet is a perfect Mother's Day gift.

YOU WILL NEED

20 cake balls, see pages 5–6
20 lollipop sticks
Bowl
Spoon
Styrofoam block
Plastic rolling pin
2 x 1½-inch (5 x 3.5-cm)
    oval cutter
Toothpick
4-inch (10-cm) flower-shape cutter
Knife

DECORATION

1 bag of yellow candy melts
1 bag of pink candy melts
Yellow sugar sprinkles
1 lb (500 g) rolled fondant in
    a selection of pretty colors
Cornstarch

DIFFICULTY RATING

PREPARE AHEAD When rolling the balls, roll half the cake balls into tulip shapes by angling your hands while rolling—you want to achieve an upside-down strawberry shape. Chill all the cake balls in the refrigerator for 1 hour.

TO MAKE THE CAKE POPS Melt the yellow candy melts (see page 6), dip 10 sticks into the melted candy, and push about halfway through the round cake balls. Melt the pink candy melts, dip the remaining sticks, and push about halfway through the tulip shapes—from the larger end. Let set. Dip the tulip cake pops into the melted pink candy and tap off the excess. Stand upright to dry. For the other flowers, dip the remaining cake pops into the melted yellow candy and sprinkle all over with yellow sugar sprinkles before the candy melt dries (over a bowl to catch the excess, which can then be sprinkled with a spoon).

Roll out your chosen colors of fondant to approximately ⅛ inch (2.5 mm) thick on a surface dusted with cornstarch.

FOR THE TULIPS Cut out six fondant ovals per cake pop. Apply pink candy melt to the bottom two-thirds of each oval using a toothpick. Stick three ovals around a tulip pop then layer the remaining three over the joints. Slightly bend out the top of the petals. Repeat with the other tulips.

FOR THE OTHER FLOWERS Cut out 10 large flower shapes. Use a knife to cut a ¾-inch (1.5-cm) slit at the dip of each petal and make a hole in the middle using a lollipop stick. Apply melted yellow candy around the hole using a toothpick and slide a fondant flower shape up the stick of each yellow cake pop, sticking it to the underside. Tip the pop upside down and neatly overlap the petals. Flip the right way around, holding in place with your hand, and secure the bottom two-thirds of the petals with candy melt. Bend out the top of the petals to create the flower shape.

SUMMER DRESS POPS

Make your favorite summer dress into a cake pop. You can change the colors of the candy melts and rolled fondant to suit your own style.

YOU WILL NEED

20 cake balls, see pages 5–6
20 lollipop sticks
Styrofoam block
Plastic rolling pin
½-inch (1-cm) heart-shape cutter
Knife
Toothpick

DECORATION

1 bag of yellow or pink candy melts
3½ oz (100 g) pink or purple rolled fondant
Cornstarch
Flower sprinkles

DIFFICULTY RATING

PREPARE AHEAD Make the cake balls into dress shapes by rolling into a fat sausage and flattening slightly. Pinch in the waist using your fingers and flare out the bottom of the dress. You may find it useful to push the bottom edge against a work surface or flat edge of a knife to create a flat bottom. Give the top some definition by adding a groove to the top edge. Chill in the refrigerator for 1 hour.

TO MAKE THE CAKE POPS Melt the yellow or pink candy melts (see page 6), dip a stick into the melted candy, and push into the bottom of a dress shape. Repeat with all the sticks and dress shapes. Let set. Dip the cake pops into the melted candy and tap off the excess. Let dry upright.

TO DECORATE Roll out the fondant to about ⅛ inch (2.5 mm) thick on a surface dusted with cornstarch. To create a belt, use a knife to cut a thin strip and attach around the waist using the melted candy and applying with a toothpick. Make a bow by cutting two heart shapes from the rolled fondant and rolling a small ball for the knot. Again, attach with the candy melt using a toothpick. Add your chosen sprinkles in the same way.

TIP
—

To remove any excess cornstarch from the fondant, gently paint on a little vodka once the fondant has hardened. The vodka will evaporate, leaving a clean finish.

BRIGHT BALLOON POPS

Bold, bright, and so simple to make.

YOU WILL NEED

20 cake balls, see pages 5–6
20 lollipop sticks
Styrofoam block
Toothpick
Styrofoam block

DECORATION

Bags of candy melts in a selection
  of bright colors
7 oz (200 g) brightly colored rolled
  fondant to match your chosen
  candy melt
Edible lacquer spray

DIFFICULTY RATING

PREPARE AHEAD Roll the cake balls into balloon shapes by angling your hands to make a point at one end. Chill in the refrigerator for 1 hour.

TO MAKE THE CAKE POPS Melt your chosen candy melts (see page 6), dip a stick into the melted candy, and push into the point of a balloon shape. Repeat with all the sticks and balloon shapes. Let set. Dip each cake pop into the melted candy, tap off the excess, and place to dry in a Styrofoam block.

TO FINISH Tear off small pea-size pieces of your chosen color of fondant to make the balloon knots. Roll the pieces into cone shapes with your hands, then attach one to each cake pop by pushing the lollipop stick all the way through from the point down. Slide the cone shape up the stick and attach to the underside of the cake pop using melted candy dabbed on with a toothpick. Roll a toothpick around the fondant to create the effect of a knot, leaving a round rim at the bottom of the cone.

Spray with edible lacquer spray to produce a shiny finish.

TIP
—

You could add numbers or names to the balloons, giving a personal touch for a children's party. Use the piping technique seen on other designs, or paint on using edible paint or powder.

PARTY HAT POPS

Bright, colorful, and playful party hats that children will have loads of fun making.

YOU WILL NEED

20 cake balls, see pages 5–6
20 lollipop sticks
Styrofoam block
Toothpick
2 plastic pastry bags
Plastic rolling pin
Knife

DECORATION

Bags of candy melts in your
    chosen colors
2 oz (50 g) brightly colored
    rolled fondant
Bright candy sequins
Large candy stars
Cornstarch

DIFFICULTY RATING

PREPARE AHEAD Form the cake balls into cone shapes by rolling at an angle against the work surface. Flatten the bottom of each shape by pushing against the work surface. Chill in the refrigerator for 1 hour.

TO MAKE THE CAKE POPS Melt your chosen candy melts (see page 6), dip a stick into the melted candy, and push about halfway through the cone shape from the flat bottom. Repeat with all the sticks and cone shapes. Let set. Dip each cake pop into the melted candy, tap off the excess, and dry upright in a Styrofoam block.

TO DECORATE Roll small balls from your chosen fondant and attach to the top of each hat, using melted candy and a toothpick. Attach the candy sequins and stars, again using the melted candy applied with a toothpick.

For the more complex striped design, fill two plastic pastry bags with contrasting colors of candy melt. Twist the tops and snip off small openings at the bottom. Pipe straight lines from the top to the bottom of a hat. Finish with a band around the bottom made by rolling the fondant to approximately $\frac{1}{16}$ inch (1.2 mm) thick on a surface dusted with cornstarch and cutting a thin strip with a knife. Attach the strip to the bottom of the hat with melted candy and a toothpick.

TEA SET POPS

Anyone for tea?

20 cake balls, see pages 5–6
20 lollipop sticks
Wax paper
Plastic rolling pin
1-inch and 2-inch (2.5-cm and
   5-cm) round cookie cutters
Small ramekin or bowl
Knife
Toothpick
½-inch (1-cm) heart-shape cutter

DECORATION

1 bag of white candy melts
11½ oz (350 g) rolled fondant in
   a color or colors of your choice
Cornstarch

DIFFICULTY RATING

PREPARE AHEAD Divide the cake balls according to how many teacups and teapots you want to make. Set the cake balls for the teapots aside. For the teacups, flatten the tops of the balls by pushing against the work surface, then slightly flatten the bottoms to let the cups stand. Chill all the shapes in the refrigerator for 1 hour.

TO MAKE THE CAKE POPS Melt the candy melts (see page 6), dip a stick into the melted candy, and push into the top of a cake shape. Repeat with all the sticks and shapes. Let set. Dip each cake pop into the melted candy and tap off the excess. Stand on wax paper so that they dry with flat bottoms. Once set, carefully peel the pops from the paper to avoid damaging the coating.

TO MAKE THE SAUCERS Roll out your chosen color of fondant to about ¹⁄₈ inch (2.5 mm) thick on a surface dusted with cornstarch. Cut out round shapes using the larger round cutter and let dry in the bottom of a small ramekin or bowl to create a curved shape.

TO MAKE THE DECORATIONS Roll the remaining fondant a little thinner. For the handles, use a knife to cut thin strips approximately ¼ x 2½ inches (5 mm x 6 cm) and fold each into a loop, securing the ends with melted candy.

Use the smaller round cutter to cut fondant circles for the teapot lids and make a hole in the center of each with a lollipop stick. Roll a small ball for the top of each teapot lid, pushing a hole through the middle with a lollipop stick. Make the teapot spouts by rolling fondant into sausage shapes. Bend into shape, then let harden slightly before attaching to the cake pop. Next, cut out the hearts from the rolled fondant. You will need five per teacup and two per teapot.

TO ASSEMBLE THE TEA SET Attach the decorations using the melted candy applied with a toothpick. Begin with the handles, hearts, and spouts, then slide the lid elements down the stick to secure on the top of the teapot cake pops. Finally, stick the bottom of each teacup to a saucer with the melted candy.

COCKTAIL POPS

Turn your favorite drink into your favorite cake pop.

YOU WILL NEED

20 cake balls, see pages 5–6
20 lollipop sticks
Styrofoam block
Knife
Medium paintbrush
Toothpick
Bowl

DECORATION

1 bag of pink or white candy melts
White, lime green, and bright blue
    sugar sprinkles
3 oz (75 g) each of red, dark green,
    lime green, and yellow rolled
    fondant
Edible glue

DIFFICULTY RATING

PREPARE AHEAD Form the cake balls into cones by rolling at an angle in your hands. Flatten the sides by rolling against a work surface and flatten the top of each cone in the same way. Chill in the refrigerator for 1 hour.

TO MAKE THE CAKE POPS Set 20 candy melt disks aside. Melt the remaining pink or white candy melts (see page 6), dip a stick into the melted candy, and push about halfway through a cone shape from the pointed end of the cone. Repeat with all the sticks and cone shapes. Let set.

Make a hole in the center of each saved candy melt disk with a knife using a screwlike motion. You will find it easiest to start on the curved side, then flip over the disk and work from the other side. Use a lollipop stick to finish the hole and make sure it's the right size. Slide the disk a third of the way up the stick. Dip the cake pop into the melted candy, coating a third of the stick as you dip. Tap off the excess and quickly push up the disk to meet the candy on the stick to set it in place. Dry in a Styrofoam block. Once dry, paint edible glue where you would like the sugar sprinkles to stick and sprinkle them on (over a bowl to catch the excess, which can then be sprinkled with a spoon).

MAKE THE GARNISHES Using fondant in different colors:

For the strawberry, make a strawberry shape out of red fondant using your fingers and slice this in half. On the curved side use a toothpick to create seedlike marks and attach a tiny piece of dark green fondant for the stalk. For the lime, shape a flat disk of lime green fondant using your fingers and remove a section with a knife so it will fit on the side of the "glass." Use a toothpick and the white melted candy to add the lines radiating from the center. For the lemon, shape a flat disk with the yellow fondant and remove a section with a knife so it will fit on the side of the glass. For the cherry, roll some red fondant into a ball.

Attach the garnishes to the cocktails using the melted candy and a toothpick.

COWGIRL HAT POPS

Perfect for a girlie party ... let's go, girls!

YOU WILL NEED

20 cake balls, see pages 5–6
20 lollipop sticks
Styrofoam block
2-inch (5-cm) round cookie cutter
Plastic rolling pin
Toothpick
Small paintbrush
Plate to mix the glitter glaze on

DECORATION

1 bag of pink candy melts
11½ oz (350 g) pink rolled fondant
Cornstarch
20 large red candy hearts
Edible pink glitter mixed with a
    little vodka

DIFFICULTY RATING

PREPARE AHEAD Form each cake ball into the top of the hat by first rolling into an egg shape. Flatten both top and bottom against the work surface and make a dip in the narrower end for the top. Chill in the refrigerator for 1 hour.

TO MAKE THE CAKE POPS Melt the candy melts (see page 6), dip a stick into the melted candy, and push about halfway through a cake shape from the flat bottom. Repeat with all the sticks and shapes. Let set. Dip each cake pop into the melted candy, tap off the excess, and set to dry in a Styrofoam block.

For the hat rims, roll out the fondant to approximately ¼ inch (5 mm) thick on a surface dusted with cornstarch and cut out 20 circles using a round cutter. Roll the circles to make them a little bigger and about ⅛ inch (2.5 mm) thick. Push a hole through the middle of each and slide up the stick to meet the cake pop. Attach using the melted candy applied with a toothpick and gently rest each hat upside down so that the fondant can dry in a drooped shape over the hat. This will give the sides a turned-up look when the pop is the right way around.

TO FINISH Attach a candy heart to the front of each hat with melted candy. Paint the heart and the edge of the hat rim using edible glitter mixed to a thick paste with a little vodka (the vodka will evaporate, leaving a clean finish).

MR. & MRS. POPS

These are a lovely alternative to the traditional wedding favor.

YOU WILL NEED

20 cake balls, see pages 5–6
20 lollipop sticks
Wax paper
Styrofoam block
Plastic pastry bag
Plastic rolling pin
Knife
Toothpick

DECORATION

1 bag of white candy melts
1 bag of black candy melts
Small piece of white rolled fondant
Small piece of black rolled fondant
Candy pearls
Edible luster spray

DIFFICULTY RATING

PREPARE AHEAD Chill the cake balls in the refrigerator for 1 hour.

TO MAKE THE CAKE POPS Melt the white candy melts (see page 6), dip a stick into the melted candy, and push into the top of a cake ball—these cake pops will be standing with the pop at the bottom of the stick, so pushing the stick into the top of the cake ball will create a slightly flat bottom. Repeat with all the sticks and cake balls. Let set. Dip the cake pops into the melted candy and tap off the excess.

For "Mrs. Pop," stand half the cake pops on a sheet of wax paper and let set—you may need to hold in place to stop it from sliding. For "Mr. Pop," allow the remaining pops to dry upside down in a Styrofoam block. Melt the black candy melts. Tilt the bowl so you can gently dip in each "Mr. Pop" at an angle to create his suit. Tap off the excess, then turn and repeat to create the other side. Let dry alongside the "Mrs. Pops" on the wax paper. Carefully peal the pops from the paper once set to avoid damaging the coating.

TO FINISH "MRS. POP" Fill a pastry bag with some of the melted white candy. Twist the top and snip off a small opening at the bottom. Pipe a V shape onto each "Mrs. Pop" and then pipe flowers by looping the candy from a central point. This will create a lacy effect. Dot some melted candy around her neck and attach the candy pearls. Finish with a spray of edible luster spray.

TO FINISH "MR. POP" Roll out the black fondant and cut into a tie shape using a knife. Attach to "Mr. Pop" using the melted white candy applied with a toothpick. To make a collar, roll out the white fondant and cut two small triangles with a knife. Attach to the neck of each pop using the melted white candy.

TIP

The pops can be adapted to suit your wedding color plan by using candy pearls in different colors for the necklace and fondant in different colors for the tie.

WEDDING CAKE POPS

A great alternative to the traditional wedding cake, these would also make cute favors for your guests.

YOU WILL NEED

1 quantity mixed cake and frosting ready to make into cake pops, see pages 5–6
Plastic rolling pin
1-inch (2.5-cm), 1¼-inch (3-cm), and 1½-inch (3.5-cm) fluted pastry cutters
20 lollipop sticks
Styrofoam block
Toothpick
Plate to mix the powder paste on
Small paintbrush

DECORATION

1 bag of white candy melts
Heart sprinkles
Royal icing flowers
Powdered food coloring in pretty colors mixed into a paste with vodka

DIFFICULTY RATING

PREPARE AHEAD Take the cake and frosting mixture and split into two (this will make it easier to roll). Roll out each piece to approximately ¾ inch (1.5 cm) thick, and use the cutters to cut out the wedding cake layers. You will need 20 circles of each size. Chill in the refrigerator for 1 hour.

TO MAKE THE CAKE POPS Melt the candy melts (see page 6), dip a stick into the melted candy, and push all the way through the center of a large circle to leave ¼ inch (5 mm) showing through the top. Use a toothpick to put candy melt over the stick and the bottom of a medium-size circle and push this on top of the bottom layer. Use a toothpick again to put the candy melt on the bottom of a small circle and attach to the rest of the cake to make the top layer. Repeat with all the sticks and cake circles. Let set.

Dip the cake pops into the melted candy and gently tap off the excess, being careful not to dislodge any layers. Stand upright to dry.

TO DECORATE Add your chosen decorations once the cake pops are dry. To attach the sprinkles and flowers, dab melted candy onto the cake pops with a toothpick. To paint the flowers, make a paste using the powdered food coloring and vodka and use a small paintbrush to add the tiny details.

TIP
—

When constructing the cake pops, you may find a small gap between each layer of cake. This can be filled with melted candy applied with a toothpick, which will ensure you produce a smooth finish once the cake pops are dipped.

BABY CARRIAGE POPS

These super cute baby carriage pops are sure to be a hit at a baby shower or Christening.

YOU WILL NEED

20 cake balls, see pages 5–6
(because a quarter of the cake
ball will be removed, make
the balls about 1½ times the
normal golf-ball size)
Knife
20 lollipop sticks
Styrofoam block
Plastic pastry bag
Toothpick

DECORATION

1 bag of white candy melts
Colored candy pearls or sequins

DIFFICULTY RATING

PREPARE AHEAD Make the cake balls into baby carriage shapes by squashing the rolled balls flat into disks. Use a knife to remove a quarter of each disk to make the hood shape. Chill in the refrigerator for 1 hour.

TO MAKE THE CAKE POPS Melt the white candy melts (see page 6). Dip a stick into the melted candy, push into a baby carriage shape, and let set. Repeat with all the sticks and baby carriage shapes. Dip each cake pop, tap off the excess, and let dry upright.

TO DECORATE Fill the pastry bag with the remaining melted candy and twist the end to seal. Snip the end of the bag to make a small hole for the candy to flow through. Be careful not to make the hole too large because the candy will be difficult to control.

Gently squeeze the bag to begin piping. Pipe a horizontal line around the cake pop starting at the corner made by the baby carriage opening. Then pipe an adjoining line around the top rim of the opening and three lines to form the hood of the carriage.

Pipe small dots below the horizontal line and attach candy pearls or sequins.

VALENTINE'S CHAMPAGNE BOTTLE POPS

Make sure your Valentine's Day goes with a "pop" with these yummy champagne bottles.

YOU WILL NEED

20 cake balls, see pages 5–6
20 lollipop sticks
Plastic rolling pin
Styrofoam block
Knife
Toothpick
Plate to mix the powder paste on
Small paintbrush

DECORATION

1 bag of green candy melts
5 oz (150 g) white rolled fondant
Cornstarch
Edible gold paint
Black powdered food coloring mixed
    into a paste with vodka

DIFFICULTY RATING

PREPARE AHEAD Make the cake balls into champagne bottles by rolling each into a fat sausage shape and flattening the bottom by pressing against the work surface. Shape the neck of the bottle by gently thinning the top end and rolling between your fingers until it is the required length. Chill in the refrigerator for one hour.

TO MAKE THE CAKE POPS Melt the candy melts (see page 6), dip a stick into the melted candy, and push into the flat bottom of a bottle shape. Repeat with all the sticks and bottle shapes. Let set. Dip each cake pop into the melted candy, tap off the excess, and let dry upright.

Create the bottle top by rolling out the fondant to about $^1/_8$ inch (2.5 mm) thick on a surface dusted with cornstarch. Use a knife to cut out thin strips and wrap a strip around the top of each bottle, attaching with the melted candy.

TO FINISH Cut a label for each bottle from the rolled fondant, approximately 1 x ¾ inch (2.5 x 1.5 cm), and attach to the bottle with candy melt dabbed on with a toothpick.

Color the bottle top and paint a collar with edible gold paint and paint a gold heart on the label. Finish off by painting a black line around the collar using the black powder paste.

SPARKLY VALENTINE'S HEART POPS

Give your heart to someone special this Valentine's Day.

YOU WILL NEED

20 cake balls, see pages 5–6
   (make the balls 1¼ times the
   normal golf-ball size)
2¼-inch (5.5-cm) heart-shape
   cookie cutter
20 lollipop sticks
Styrofoam block
Bowl
Spoon
Styrofoam block

DECORATION

1 bag of red candy melts
Red sprinkles
Edible red glitter (add a touch of this
   to the sprinkles to give an extra
   sparkle to your finish)

DIFFICULTY RATING

PREPARE AHEAD Take the cake balls (these are made slightly larger than normal to ensure the heart is thick enough to push the stick into) and push into the heart cutter, making sure that you reach all areas of the underside. Smooth over the top as best you can to produce a flat finish and gently release the cake from the cutter. Chill in the refrigerator for 1 hour.

TO MAKE THE CAKE POPS Melt the candy melts (see page 6), dip a stick into the melted candy, and push about halfway through a heart from the pointed end. Lightly pinch each side of the heart as you do this to stop the cake from cracking. Repeat with all the sticks and hearts. Let set.

Dip each cake pop into the melted candy, tap off the excess, and immediately sprinkle all over with the combined red sprinkles and glitter (over a bowl to catch the excess, which can then be sprinkled with a spoon). Stand in a Styrofoam block to dry.

TIP

If cracks do appear on the cake hearts before dipping, fill them with melted candy applied with a toothpick.

CHOCOLATE EASTER EGG POPS

Make these with the rich chocolate cake and frosting for an
alternative Easter treat.

YOU WILL NEED

20 cake balls, see pages 5–6
20 lollipop sticks
Wax paper
Toothpick

DECORATION

1 bag of light cocoa candy melts
Brightly colored candy sequins

DIFFICULTY RATING

PREPARE AHEAD Roll the cake balls into egg shapes by angling your hands
while rolling. Chill in the refrigerator for 1 hour.

TO MAKE THE CAKE POPS Melt the candy melts (see page 6), dip a
stick into the melted candy, and push into the top of an egg shape. Repeat with all
the sticks and egg shapes. Let set. Dip each cake pop into the melted candy, tap off
the excess, and place onto the wax paper, holding in place until dry.

TO DECORATE Attach the candy sequins to the eggs in a random fashion
using the melted candy dabbed on with a toothpick.

TIP
—

These cake pops could easily be made the other way around, with the egg at the
top of the stick. Try wrapping them individually in cellophane bags—they would
make delicious Easter gifts.

SPARKLY PUMPKIN POPS

Superbright, sparkly pumpkins are great trick-or-treat gifts.

YOU WILL NEED

20 cake balls, see pages 5–6
Spoon
20 lollipop sticks
Styrofoam block
Bowl

DECORATION

1 bag of orange candy melts
Orange sugar sprinkles
Green jelly beans, cut in half

DIFFICULTY RATING

PREPARE AHEAD Add grooves to each cake ball by rolling the edge of a spoon handle down the side from top to bottom. The grooves will need to be deep to make sure they show through the candy melt. Chill in the refrigerator for 1 hour.

TO MAKE THE CAKE POPS Melt the candy melts (see page 6), dip a stick into the melted candy, and push into a cake ball. Repeat with all the sticks and cake balls. Let set.

Dip each cake pop into the melted candy and tap off the excess. While still wet, sprinkle all over with the orange sugar sprinkles (over a bowl to catch the excess, which can then be sprinkled with a spoon) and push a jelly bean halfway into the top to create the stalk. Let dry upright.

TIP
—

To create a spooky pumpkin, you could omit the sprinkles and just coat the cake pops in the orange candy melts to leave a smooth finish. Create a ghoulish face using powdered food coloring mixed with a little vodka and a small paintbrush.

BAT POPS

Cute yet spooky, these wacky pops are sure to be a hit at any Halloween party.

YOU WILL NEED

20 cake balls, see pages 5–6
20 lollipop sticks
Styrofoam block
Plastic rolling pin
1¼-inch (3-cm) heart-shape cutter
Knife
Toothpick

DECORATION

1 bag of black candy melts
11 oz (325 g) black rolled fondant
Cornstarch
40 white candy sequins
20 small orange candy sequins

DIFFICULTY RATING

PREPARE AHEAD Chill the cake balls in the refrigerator for 1 hour.

TO MAKE THE CAKE POPS Melt the candy melts (see page 6), dip a stick into the melted candy, and push into a cake ball. Repeat with all the sticks and cake balls. Let set. Dip each cake pop into the melted candy, tap off the excess, and let dry upright.

TO MAKE THE BAT WINGS AND EARS Roll out the black fondant to approximately ⅛ inch (2.5 mm) thick on a surface dusted with cornstarch and cut out 40 heart shapes. Cut off a crescent shape from each heart so the wing will fit onto the side of the bat. Let the hearts dry and become firm.

Make the bat ears by flattening small cone shapes of black fondant.

TO ASSEMBLE THE BATS Use the melted black candy and a toothpick to attach the wings to each side of the cake ball and the ears between the top of the wings. Attach white sequins as eyes and an orange sequin as a nose. Then dot a small amount of melted black candy into the center of the white sequins to finish off the eyes.

TIP
—

Hold the cake pop on its side while attaching each wing to help it set straight.

STOCKING POPS

Get creative with your stocking decorations to make these pops fit in with your Christmas decorations.

20 cake balls, see pages 5–6
20 lollipop sticks
Styrofoam block
Spoon
Bowl
Toothpick

DECORATION

1 bag of red candy melts
1 bag of green candy melts
¼ bag of white candy melts
Red, green, and white sugar sprinkles
Large star sprinkles
Large snowflake sprinkles

DIFFICULTY RATING

PREPARE AHEAD Form the cake balls into stockings by rolling each into a sausage shape and bending the end around to create the toe. Flatten off the top edge by pressing against the work surface. Chill in the refrigerator for 1 hour.

TO MAKE THE CAKE POPS Melt your selected color of candy melts (see page 6), dip the stick into the melted candy, and push into the heel of the stocking. Repeat with all the sticks and stocking shapes. Let set. Dip each cake pop into the melted candy, tap off the excess, and let dry upright.

Melt the contrasting color candy. Use a large spoon to hold some of the candy melt and dip the rim of each stocking, then sprinkle with matching sugar sprinkles while wet (over a bowl to catch the excess, which can then be sprinkled with a spoon). Repeat with the toe of the stocking and let dry.

TO DECORATE Attach your chosen festive sprinkles onto the side of the stocking using the matching melted candy applied with a toothpick.

CHRISTMAS CRACKER POPS

Add a touch of merry old England to your Christmas table and have a delicious after-dinner treat.

YOU WILL NEED

20 cake balls, see pages 5–6
20 lollipop sticks
Styrofoam block
Small paintbrush
Toothpick

DECORATION

1 bag of red candy melts
Edible gold paint
40 large star sprinkles

DIFFICULTY RATING

PREPARE AHEAD Form the cake balls into crackers—like hard candies in wrappers—by rolling each ball into a sausage shape. Flatten off the ends by pushing against the work surface. Use a lollipop stick to push grooves into the sausage about ½ inch (1 cm) from each end and use a pinching action to spread out the ends to produce a cracker shape. Chill in the refrigerator for 1 hour.

TO MAKE THE CAKE POPS Melt the candy melts (see page 6), dip a stick into the melted candy, and push into the middle of a cracker shape. Repeat with all the sticks and crackers. Let set. Dip each cake pop into the melted candy, tap off the excess, and let dry upright.

TO DECORATE Paint a zigzag pattern around the ends of each cracker with edible gold paint.

Attach a large star to each side of the cracker using candy melt and a toothpick. Paint each star gold.

TIP
—

Why not try this design in a variety of festive colors and patterns?

TEDDY BEAR POPS

Everybody will love these sweet little teddy bears.

YOU WILL NEED

20 cake balls, see pages 5–6
20 lollipop sticks
Styrofoam block
Plastic rolling pin
½-inch (1-cm) and ¾-inch (1.5-cm) round cookie cutters
¼-inch (5-mm) heart-shape cutter
Knife
Toothpick
Plate to mix the powder paste on
Small paintbrush

DECORATION

1 bag of light cocoa candy melts
40 candy-coated chocolates
2 oz (50 g) light brown rolled fondant
1 oz (25 g) black rolled fondant
Cornstarch
Black powdered food coloring mixed into a paste with vodka

DIFFICULTY RATING

PREPARE AHEAD Chill the cake balls in the refrigerator for 1 hour.

TO MAKE THE CAKE POPS Melt the light cocoa candy melts (see page 6), dip a stick in the melted candy, and push into a cake ball. To attach the ears, dip a candy-coated chocolate halfway and push it against the cake ball. Hold until set, then repeat to make the other ear. Repeat with all the sticks, cake balls, and candy-coated chocolates.

Dip each cake pop in the melted candy, tap off the excess, and let dry upright.

TO FINISH Roll out the light brown fondant to ¹/₈ inch (2.5 mm) thick on a surface that has been dusted with cornstarch. Use the round cutters to cut out two small circles and one larger circle per bear. Cut the smaller circles with a knife, making a straight edge to fit inside the ears and attach using melted candy applied with a toothpick.

Attach the larger circle to the middle of each bear face using the melted candy.

Roll out the black fondant to ¹/₈ inch (2.5 mm) thick on a surface that has been dusted with cornstarch. Use the small heart cutter to cut out 20 hearts and attach to the circle using the melted candy.

Paint on eyes, nose, and mouth using the black powder paste.

TIP

These teddy bears would look great in different colors, too.

PENGUIN POPS

We just love these penguin pops!

YOU WILL NEED

20 cake balls, see pages 5–6
20 lollipop sticks
Styrofoam block
Spoon
Plastic rolling pin
½-inch (1-cm) and 1¼-inch (3-cm)
   heart-shape cutters
Small triangle cutter
Knife
Toothpick

DECORATION

1 bag of black candy melts
¼ bag of white candy melts
5 oz (150 g) black rolled fondant
5 oz (150 g) orange rolled fondant
Cornstarch
40 white candy sequins

DIFFICULTY RATING

PREPARE AHEAD Chill the cake balls in the refrigerator for 1 hour.

TO MAKE THE CAKE POPS Melt the black candy melts (see page 6), dip a stick into the melted candy, and push into a cake ball. Repeat with all the sticks and cake balls. Let set. Dip each cake pop in the melted candy, tap off the excess, and let dry upright in a Styrofoam block.

Melt the white candy melts and take a large spoonful. Dip the front of each cake pop into the spoon to make the penguin's belly. Tap off a little excess, then gently tap the pop the other way around to create a smooth belly. Let dry.

TO MAKE THE WINGS, FEET, AND BEAKS Roll out the black fondant to approximately ⅛ inch (2.5 mm) thick on a surface dusted with cornstarch and cut out 40 large heart shapes for the wings.

Roll out the orange fondant and cut 40 smaller hearts for the feet. Then cut 20 small orange triangles for the beaks—trim the triangles to the correct size using a knife.

TO ASSEMBLE THE PENGUINS Use the black melted candy and a toothpick to attach beak, feet, and wings. Leave the wings loose at the bottom and push out slightly. Attach white candy sequins for eyes and dot the centers with black melted candy.

TIP
—

Add a little gum tragacanth (approximately 2 teaspoons per handful of fondant) to the fondant and mix in well. This will give the fondant a firmer texture, which will help it to hold the desired shape.

DUCK FAMILY POPS

Let your imagination run wild and create your own selection of mad and funky ducks.

20 cake balls, see pages 5–6
20 lollipop sticks
Plastic rolling pin
Styrofoam block
¾-inch (1.5-cm) round
   cookie cutter
Knife
Toothpick
Plate to mix the powder paste on
Small paintbrush
¼-inch (5-mm), ½-inch (1-cm),
   ¾-inch (1.5-cm), and 1-inch
   (2.5-cm) heart-shape cutters
¾-inch (1.5-cm) flower-shape cutter

DECORATION

1 bag of yellow or pink candy melts
7 oz (200 g) orange rolled fondant
   plus small pieces of other colors
Cornstarch
Black powdered food coloring mixed
   into a paste with vodka
Yellow candy sequins
Heart sprinkles

DIFFICULTY RATING

PREPARE AHEAD Split each cake ball into two pieces, one three times larger than the other. Roll each smaller piece into a ball to make the head and make each larger piece into a body by rolling into a ball, flattening the bottom, and creating a point at one end for the tail. Chill in the refrigerator for 1 hour.

TO MAKE THE CAKE POPS Melt the yellow or pink candy melts (see page 6), dip a stick into the melted candy, and push into the flat bottom of a body section. Dip the bottom of a head into the melted candy and attach to the body, hold in place until set. Repeat with all the sticks, bodies, and heads. Dip each cake pop into the melted candy and tap off the excess. Let dry upright.

TO ADD BEAKS AND EYES Roll out the orange fondant to approximately ¹/₈ inch (2.5 mm) thick on a surface dusted with cornstarch and cut out 20 circles. Cut each circle with a knife just over halfway down to create a beak shape. Attach using the melted candy applied with a toothpick. Paint on the eyes using the black powder paste.

TO FINISH Add decorations of your choice to complete the design, using melted candy applied with a toothpick to attach them.

Create the bows and bow tie from colored rolled fondant, cutting two small hearts (smallest size for the bow tie) and rolling a tiny ball for the knot.

Cut out flower shapes from rolled fondant, and add a candy sequin to the center.

For the Mohican, trim the point from three heart sprinkles and attach with the melted candy.

For each set of wings, cut out four hearts, two ¾ inch (1.5 cm) and two 1 inch (2.5 cm), from rolled fondant and layer them on each side of the duck, attaching with the melted candy.

WHALE POPS

You'll have a whale of a time making this pop!

20 cake balls, see pages 5–6
20 lollipop sticks
Styrofoam block
Knife
Toothpick
Plate to mix the powder paste on
Small paintbrush

DECORATION

1 bag of blue candy melts
3½ oz (100 g) blue rolled fondant
40 white candy sequins
Black powdered food coloring mixed
   into a paste with vodka

DIFFICULTY RATING

PREPARE AHEAD Shape the cake balls into whales by first rolling them into egg shapes. Shape a tail by pinching each cake from the narrower end, gently pulling it outward, and flattening a little. Split the end into two, fan outward, and finish by curving the tail upward. Chill in the refrigerator for 1 hour.

TO MAKE THE CAKE POPS Melt the candy melts (see page 6), dip a stick into the melted candy, and push into the underside of a whale shape. Repeat with all the sticks and shapes. Let set. Dip each cake pop into the melted candy, tap off the excess, and stand in a Styrofoam block to dry.

TO FINISH Make the water spurt by taking a little blue rolled fondant, roll it into a sausage, and split it from about halfway down using the knife. Bend the ends outward and attach to the top of each whale using the melted candy and a toothpick.

Add two white candy sequins to the side of each whale's head using the melted candy and paint on eyes and a wide smile with black powder paste.

TIP
—

Don't worry if the tail cracks as you are shaping it because the cracks can be filled with melted candy, applied with a toothpick, before you dip the cake pop.

PARROT POPS

Cuteness with a tropical twist!

YOU WILL NEED

20 cake balls, see pages 5–6
20 lollipop sticks
Styrofoam block
Small paintbrush
Plastic rolling pin
¼-inch (5-mm) heart-shape cutter
Toothpick
Plate to mix the powder paste on
Small paintbrush

DECORATION

1 bag of blue candy melts
1 bag of red candy melts
¼ bag of yellow candy melts
   (for red parrot only)
Small piece of black rolled fondant
Cornstarch
40 white candy sequins
Black powdered food coloring mixed
   into a paste with vodka

DIFFICULTY RATING

PREPARE AHEAD Remove a small, pea-size piece from each cake ball for the beak. Form the cake balls into parrot shapes by first rolling into fat sausages. Use your thumb to push down the tail and make the head end slightly narrower than the belly of the parrot. Form each small piece into a curved, pointed beak with a flat bottom that will fit on the head of the parrot. Chill in the refrigerator for 1 hour.

TO MAKE THE CAKE POPS Melt the blue or red candy melts (see page 6), dip a stick into the melted candy, and push into a parrot shape underneath the belly. Dip the flat part of the beak into the candy melt and attach to the front of the parrot head. Repeat with all the sticks, parrot shapes, and beaks. Let set. Dip each cake pop into the melted candy, tap off the excess, and stand in a Styrofoam block to dry.

TO FINISH Melt the yellow candy and paint a wing onto each side of the red parrot's body. Let this dry, then paint over the lower section with the blue candy melt.

To make the feet, roll out the black fondant to approximately ⅛ inch (2.5 mm) thick on a surface dusted with cornstarch and cut out 40 heart shapes. Attach these and the white sequins for eyes using melted candy and a toothpick.

Use the black powder paste to paint on the black features—the beaks, eyes, and the wings for the blue parrot.

PIGGY POPS

Piggy perfection!

YOU WILL NEED

20 cake balls, see pages 5–6
20 lollipop sticks
Styrofoam block
Toothpick
Plate to mix the powder paste on
Small paintbrush

DECORATION

1 bag of pink candy melts
3½ oz (100 g) pink rolled fondant
Black powdered food coloring mixed
    into a paste with vodka

DIFFICULTY RATING

PREPARE AHEAD Chill the cake balls in the refrigerator for 1 hour.

TO MAKE THE CAKE POPS Melt the pink candy melts (see page 6), dip a stick into the melted candy, and push into a cake ball. Repeat with all the sticks and cake balls. Let set. Dip each cake pop into the melted candy, tap off the excess, and let dry upright.

TO MAKE EARS AND SNOUTS Roll 40 small pieces of pink rolled fondant into small cones and flatten slightly to make the ears. Take a larger piece to form each snout by rolling into a ball, flattening slightly, and rolling on its edge to make a flat cylindrical shape. Attach ears and snouts using melted candy applied with a toothpick.

TO FINISH Paint on the eyes, nostrils, and smile using the black powder paste.

CATERPILLAR POPS

This caterpillar pop design is perfect for children's parties because you can add a message, such as "Happy Birthday," to the body.

YOU WILL NEED

20 cake balls (or however many you need for your chosen body length), see pages 5–6
20 lollipop sticks
Styrofoam block
Toothpick
Plate to mix the powder paste on
Small paintbrush

DECORATION

1 bag of blue candy melts
1 bag of yellow candy melts
2 mini marshmallows
2 green candy-coated chocolate chips
2 white hard candy disks (as used in candy bracelets)
2 black candy pearls
Black powdered food coloring mixed into a paste with vodka

DIFFICULTY RATING

PREPARE AHEAD Chill the cake balls in the refrigerator for 1 hour.

TO MAKE THE CAKE POPS Melt the blue and yellow candy melts (see page 6), dip a stick in your chosen color of melted candy, and push into a cake ball. Repeat with all the sticks and cake balls. Let set. Dip each cake pop into the melted candy, tap off the excess, and dry upright in a Styrofoam block.

FOR THE HEAD Attach two mini marshmallows to the top of one of the cake pops using the melted candy and a toothpick, then attach a candy-coated chocolate chip to the top of each marshmallow. Add the two white hard candy disks to the front of the head and place a black candy pearl in the middle of each, securing it with the melted candy. Finally, paint on a large smile using the black powder paste.

TIP

To personalize the caterpillar with a birthday message or name, either use the piping technique (see page 7) or paint using brightly colored powdered food coloring mixed to a paste with a little vodka.

CONVERSIONS

1 teaspoon = 5 ml
1 tablespoon = 15 ml

For those who cook with gas, the temperature conversion you will require when baking the basic cake recipe is:

350°F/180°C/Gas Mark 4

GLOSSARY

Confectioners' sugar = icing sugar
Cornstarch = cornflour
Edible lacquer spray = edible glaze spray
Pastry bag = piping bag
Rolled fondant = ready-to-roll icing
Royal icing flower = sugar flower
Self-rising flour = self-raising flour
Styrofoam = polystyrene
Superfine sugar = caster sugar
Toothpick = cocktail stick
Wax paper = greaseproof paper

SOURCE LIST

Check out our website www.popcakekitchen.co.uk for your cake-pop making needs. We sell lollipop sticks, bags, twist ties, and candy melts. We also have popcake kits to help you get started.

Internet sources for decorating ingredients and sugarcraft equipment supplies. Many of the companies also have retail locations.

UK

The Cake Decorating Company
Online supplier
Tel. 0115 822 4521
www.thecakedecoratingcompany.co.uk

Cakes Cookies and Crafts Shop
Online supplier
Tel. 01524 389 684
www.cakescookiesandcraftsshop.co.uk

Sugarshack
Online and retail supplier
Unit 12, Bowmans Trading Estate
Westmoreland Road
London NW9 9RL
Tel. 020 8204 2994
www.sugarshack.co.uk

Almond Art
Online supplier
Showroom: Unit 15/16, Faraday Close
Gorse Lane Industrial Estate
Clacton-on-Sea
Essex CO15 4TR
Tel. 01255 223 322
www.almondart.com

Blue Ribbons Sugarcraft Centre
Online and retail supplier
29 Walton Road, East Molesey
Surrey KT8 0DH
Tel. 020 8941 1591
www.blueribbons.co.uk

Jane Asher Party Cakes & Sugarcraft
Online and retail supplier
22–24 Cale Street
London SW3 3QU
Tel. 020 7584 6177
www.jane-asher.co.uk

Squires Shop and School
Online and retail supplier
Squires House, 3 Waverley Lane
Farnham, Surrey GU9 8BB
Tel. 0845 61 71 810
www.squires-group.co.uk

USA

Candy Direct, Inc.
Online and retail supplier
745 Design Court, Suite 602
Chula Vista, CA 91911
Tel. 619-216-0116
www.candydirect.com

Global Sugar Art
Online supplier
Tel. 1-800-420-6088
www.globalsugarart.com

N.Y. Cake & Baking Dist.
Online and retail supplier
56 West 22nd Street
NY, NY 10021
Tel. 212-675-CAKE
www.nycake.com

Pfeil & Holing
Online supplier
Tel. 1-800-247-7955
www.cakedeco.com

Sweet Factory
Online and retail supplier
Tel: 562-391-2410
www.sweetfactory.com

Wilton Homewares Store
Online and retail supplier
Tel. 1-800-794-5866
www.wilton.com

CANADA

Creative Cutters
Online supplier
1-888-805-3444
www.creativecutters.com

Golda's Kitchen
Online supplier
Tel. 1-866-465-3299
www.goldaskitchen.com

AUSTRALIA & NEW ZEALAND

Cake Deco
Online and retail supplier
Shop 7, Port Phillip Arcade
232 Flinders Street, Melbourne,
Victoria, Australia
Tel. 03 9654 5335
www.cakedeco.com.au

Milly's
Online and retail supplier
273 Ponsonby Road
Auckland, New Zealand
Tel. 0800 200 123
www.millyskitchen.co.nz

SOUTH AFRICA

Kadies Bakery Supplies
Online and retail supplier
Kingfisher Shopping Centre
Kingfisher Drive
Fourways, Gauteng
South Africa
Tel. 027 11 465-5572
www.kadies.co.za

ACKNOWLEDGMENTS

My thanks go to Veronica for introducing us to the fantastic world of cake pops, and also to my parents, family, and friends, especially Kathryn and Nicole, for their continuous encouragement, belief, and support.
   Finally, to my husband, who throughout the whole process has been a huge support and inspiration, and who has kindly eaten more than his fair share of pops along the way in the quest to achieve the "perfect pop"! **HELEN**

I wish to thank my family and friends for their continuous love, support, and inspiration, especially my parents who have always filled me with the strength and belief to reach my dreams.
   An extra special thank you is for my boyfriend, Matt. I could not have done this without his encouragement, inspiration, and understanding, especially through all the late nights making pops! **ABBY**

A final special thanks to Greg, who helped in the creation and evolution of Popcake Kitchen.